PS 3570 .E6937 F57 2000
Terris, Susan.
Fire is favorable to the
 dreamer

*Fire Is Favorable to the Dreamer*

SUSAN TERRIS

ARCTOS PRESS

**Fire Is Favorable to the Dreamer**

ARCTOS PRESS

Copyright © 2003 by Susan Terris

All rights reserved. No part of this book may be reproduced or transmitted in any form or by any means, electronic or mechanical, including photocopying, recording or by an information storage and retrieval system without written permission from the author except for the inclusion of brief quotations in a review.

ISBN 0-9657015-8-1

Library of Congress Control Number: 2002113107
Library of Congress Cataloging-in-Publication Data
1. Poetry  2. Terris, Susan - Poetry
3. United States - 21st Century - Poetry

First Edition

Book design by Jeremy Thornton
Front cover and frontispiece: "The Magdalen with the Smoking Flame" (detail) by Georges de La Tour, reproduced with the permission of the Los Angeles County Museum, gift of the Ahmanson Foundation.
Back cover photograph by Diane Rosenblum Althoff

ARCTOS PRESS
P.O. Box 401
Sausalito, CA 94966-0401
CB Follett: Publisher
Runes@aol.com
http://members.aol.com/Runes

*For David, with love*

## Acknowledgments

Poems from this book appeared, some in slightly different versions, in the following journals:

*Big Bridge, Black Bear Review, Calyx, The Cape Rock, The Chiron Review, The Comstock Review, Connecticut Review, convolvulus, Disquieting Muses, Drunken Boat, 5 A.M., The Florida Review, ForPoetry.com, Free Lunch, Green Hills Literary Lantern, Highland Flyer, Jack Magazine, Kalliope, Literal Latté, Lynx Eye, The MacGuffin, Midstream, Nerve Cowboy, New Works Review, Notre Dame Review, Pedestal, Peregrine, PoetryBay, PoetryMagazine.com, Pudding Magazine, Rhino, Sheila-Na-Gig, SideReality, Small Spiral Notebook, Spoon River Poetry Review, Skidrow Penthouse, Sojourner, So to Speak, The Sun, Thema, The Westchester Writer.*

Poems from this book appeared, some in slightly different versions, in the following publications:

**Dorothy Parker's Elbow** edited by Kim Addonizio and Cheryl Dumesnil (Warner Books)
**Emily Dickinson Award Anthology** (Universities West Press)
**Eye of the Holocaust** by Susan Terris (Arctos Press)
**Heart to Heart**, edited by Jan Greenberg (Harry N. Abrams Inc.)
**Nantucket, A Collection** (Whitefish Press)

**Table of Contents**

## I. *Trespass Into Morning*

Love of Lost Time .................................................. 3
Moonrakers' Treasure ............................................. 4
Riding the Wind ..................................................... 5
River of Milky Light ................................................ 7
The Last Time This Water Saw Land,
  It Was in Africa .................................................... 8
The Poet Studies How to Make Books ..................... 9
A Sounding Hieroglyphic ...................................... 10
Trespass Into Morning .......................................... 11
How Many Bees Are There in a Day? .................... 12
1981: Sprite Lost, Sprite Found ............................. 13
Zodiacal Glow ...................................................... 14
Getting Tattooed the Hard Way ............................ 15
Let Me Tell You About the Rat-Zapper .................. 16
Immortality of Culture .......................................... 17
Fallen Light .......................................................... 18

## II. *Lady in the Cube*

Eye of the Water Lily ............................................ 23
Baggage ............................................................... 24
Seeing the Outline ................................................ 25
Lady in the Cube .................................................. 26
Vermeer's Wife / Vermeer ..................................... 27
Louise Nevelson: Architect of Shadows ................. 28
Gertrude Stein and *Picasso*: On Picasso .............. 29
The Tarot Fool Steps Into Space ............................ 30
Purple Echoes ...................................................... 31

| | |
|---|---|
| Michael Mazur: Ice Glen, 1993 | 32 |
| Archaeology of Falling | 33 |
| Illumination | 34 |
| Self-Portrait in Ink | 36 |
| Rotation to Winter | 38 |
| From the Wing Bone of a Crane | 39 |
| The Rest of the Landscape is Dim, Pleading Ignorance | 40 |

## III. *Blue Roses*

| | |
|---|---|
| Bright Princess: Moment of Impact | 45 |
| Kursk Good-Bye | 46 |
| Mary Todd Lincoln at Ford's Theatre | 48 |
| Adolf's Mother Imagines the Future | 50 |
| Holocaust Museum: Crematorium II | 51 |
| Einstein's Daughter | 52 |
| The Girl Who Flew Like a Kite | 53 |
| Breaking Away From the Family | 54 |
| Blue Roses in Angria | 55 |
| Death of a Podiatrist | 56 |
| Escaping Sodom | 57 |
| In a Jail of My Own | 58 |
| The Magician's Apprentice | 59 |
| Marilyn M. Thinks About French & Russian Dogs | 60 |
| Paramedics at the Scene of the Dog Mauling | 61 |
| Janis Says: *Burn, Baby, Burn* | 63 |
| You, Walking Out of the Ashes | 64 |

## IV. *Fire Is Favorable*

Putting Your Money Where Your Mouth Is .................. 69

Definitions of Twilight .............................................. 70

What You Want Really Want, Lady: ........................... 71

Letter & Package Bomb Indicators ............................ 72

Burnout Woman & Man of Grass .............................. 74

Avalanche Warning ................................................. 75

Moving Out ............................................................ 76

Less Velvet Ropes ................................................... 81

Fire Is Favorable to the Dreamer .............................. 82

   To Dream of Seeing a Tower Denotes
   You Will Aspire to High Elevations ......................... 82

   To Dream Your Slippers Are Much Admired
   Foretells You Will Be Involved in a Flirtation
      That Will Bring Disgrace ..................................... 83

   Fire Is Favorable to the Dreamer
   If She Doesn't Get Burned ..................................... 84

   To Dream of Black Swans Denotes Illicit Pleasures ....... 85

   To Dream of Eating Vegetables
   Is an Omen of Strange Luck .................................... 86

*Fire Is Favorable to the Dreamer*

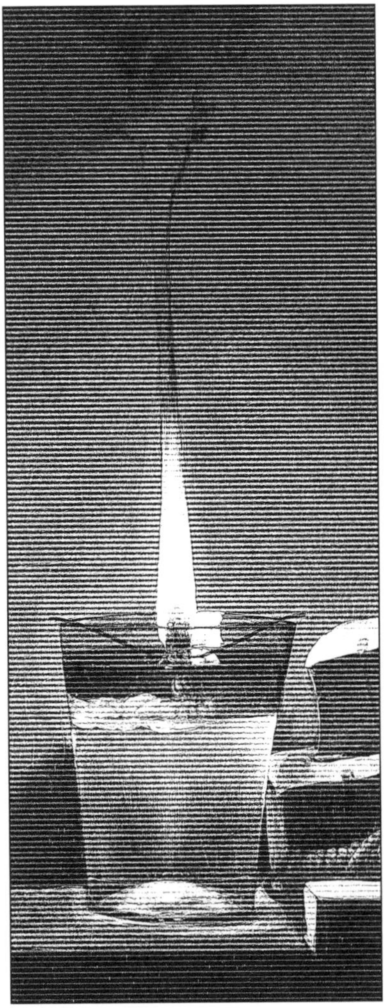

# I.

# *Trespass Into Morning*

## *Love of Lost Time*

Notice the tree of discarded leaves
bent by the river where a woman holds a line.

Metaphors hardly visible,
shadings of weight, pauses in tone,
flick of memory,
as the river yields light and motion
of current.

She never tried to triumph in whitewater
or upon sheer faces of rock.
Instead, fading pictures
where slouch and grace showed them
all without clothes,

sharing ripe fruit
as, one by one, they traded images,
dropped numbered expectations
while cast off pips
bobbed drunkenly downstream.

Love of lost time is a bottomless eddy
where her line will circle and keep on circling.

## *Moonrakers' Treasure*

In the square of window reflected on a window,
a scribble of cirrus, wave and sand, corner of an eave.
Then two pelicans make sky their movie screen.

Soon she'll watch herself walk below the eave
wearing a hat she's never seen, trailed by
an unfamiliar dog and a shadow not her own.

Odd to exist in simultaneity – a flatland image,
but she seems to have strayed from her own life
into a film scrolling across the beach house window.

Past Duxbury Reef, a three-masted sailing ship looms.
It's day-for-night and, under a waning crescent,
moonrakers scuttle like crabs across rock and sand.

She and her shadow and the nameless dog are hunched
in a dinghy rowing treasure toward the ship,
toward adventure with a captain who has

eyepatch, bagpipes, and a pirate's salty breeches.
Below decks, a beamed cabin smelling faintly of fish
and dog, where she and her shadow embrace.

She has untied herself from the every day. Now she
and her shadow, listening to skirl of bagpipe,
are at sea with the moonrakers' treasure in their arms.

## *Riding the Wind*

A woman is cradled in the dunes.  Behind her,
fleshy fingers of ice plant and the gray-green
of granite.  She draws a name in the sand,
but the wind rakes it and her untamed hair.
Time makes everything softer, harder,
and impossible to control.

∽

The child in the dune grass says the man is kind,
though kindness is not what the woman
would say.  Dangerous, perhaps, mercurial.
Or sad.  Because the man lost his wife,
the child says, he needs the woman to kiss him,
to sit with him and hold his hand
while he falls asleep.

∽

I never know what is true or what may be real.
Kisses are elusive as duned sand, as barbed
as wild roses.  They can't be held
except as a memory and are weightless arcs
of roundness and urgency, transparent,
mythical as a centaur
galloping across fringes of evening surf.

∽

The centaur leaves hoof marks in the sand,
reaches out with questing hands,
grazes the woman's brow with his lips,
inviting her to mount and straddle him,
to abandon the child, so they can
ride the wind together, heading toward
sunset and toward the promise
of a green flash.

～

At the reef, moonrakers ghost the shore
searching for treasure combed across its rocks.
Wealth is where you find it.
A hoof beat, a heartbeat, a stolen kiss.
The woman will not retrace her path.
What is lost cannot be recaptured. The wind has
stripped her but, though empty-handed,
she remembers sweet roses she wove
into the depths of
the centaur's springy mane.

## River of Milky Light

Furled in a blue dream, trimmed and wicked,
Ophelia beams through a pathless graveyard

where leaf and branch tremble with mad light
as sky-swatches drift slowly down.

Stretching up, afraid to breathe, she juggles
them on the tips of her fingers.

*Don't go away,* she whispers. *Suspense is all.*
*Tonight, everything lost must be returned.*

But while archer and huntress prowl
with a river of blue-starred light between them,

she stumbles, drops rosemary, violets, rue,
and thyme black as her shadow.

When she bends forward to seine them –
*nonny, hey nonny* – from the river, she catches

herself reflected there. Reaching out and down,
she and her mirror-image embrace:

blue-black lovers, their dreams unfurled,
wet and weightless in currents of milky light.

# *The Last Time This Water Saw Land, It Was in Africa*

The last time this parrot saw fish,
it was flying over an island purpled by sunset.
The last time this pebble skipped across
a white sand beach, it was tossed
by a man with a parrot on his shoulder
and a fish in his creel.
The last time this key saw a lock,
I was on an island with the man, the parrot, the creel,
the fish, and a hot golden ball at the horizon.
But winds were fierce, the man and the light
unforgiving. So I shook
sand from my shoes, locked my suitcase,
and caught a plane.
In my hand, one smooth pebble
and a notebook lined with Caribbean clichés.

## *The Poet Studies How to Make Books*

Duxbury Reef, a fringe on the horizon.
From above, the slow curve of the earth,
marl and loam, a bridge
across time into the high summers of the past.

*Use your bones,* the bookmaker told us.
*Instill in the paper, the memory of the fold.*

Water grooves rock. Paper holds memories.
Folds, too. Folds of now. Of then.
Of the tame or the wild. A suspension
in surf-sounds, and time seems to stop.

*Use your bones,* she said, and this feels right.
Bones can hold memory, mark a place.

Duxbury Reef at all times and seasons:
pelicans swallow fish by day as moonrakers
swallow memories at night. But time is ruptured,
and sand sifts over inked and folded pages.

# *A Sounding Hieroglyphic*

Paper scroll of days, cast aside
except when recast which seldom occurs.
I mean to unroll it, dry mount
and preserve it: acrostic of an elusive life,

but already there's a God-sky in the west,
needling discreetly through trees.
Still, the far horizon
is crayoned with unholy abandon.
Struck with wonder, I begin to count
rays with my fingers while pagan Fates
encircle this ragged matter.

As spiders will redo wind-torn webs,
the Fates will help me piece the damage.
*Trust us,* they whisper,
yet I must unpuzzle the enigma,
paste up a yellow sun
and put on yellow socks to lighten my feet.

I wait and another hour unfurls,
arch with longing,
coded in shivered symbols.
As papyrus and vellum offer up surprises,
a sounding hieroglyphic
imprints upon my ear.  Though I try
to listen, today's warm scraps of yellow
are all I can endure.

## Trespass Into Morning

Don't awaken me. I'm walking out of my night
into the dark matter of your dreams.
Pinwheels of fluorescence disguise me
as I trespass. You: hot and trusting

on your back, like a careless cat, breath faint,
your unmarked face exposing
the lie of decadence. *And so, love,*
*why am I here, and what am I meant to do?*

Olive-skinned girl and boy with blonde curls
are eyeing us. Your children? Mine?
Or ourselves thrust forward
in clothes exhausted from another life?

Hand in hand the two poise in the doorway,
watching me watching you, as pinwheels coalesce
into wings, and fireflies
rise up to stun the air between us.

## *How Many Bees Are There in a Day?*

In the air, a tinge of honey and buzz of morning,
cherry, redbud, pear rimming her glance

as she stepped from the arboretum and shook her arms
until leaves began to fall away from her body.

Lighter, stronger, less green, she inhaled sky,
its blue defaced only by dust motes, and then earth,

a place of dazzle without pain: the pond water
unclouded to match the sky, the fish uncounted.

She was naked now and pliable, dropping to knees
then to belly in spears of fat-bladed grass.

The sun ardent on her back, she stretched
and rolled – Jill without her pail – downhill

toward the storied hives,

an innocent, not yet alert to swarm and fury
or to the sure promise of sting and sting and sting.

## *1981: Sprite Lost, Sprite Found*

Liberty.  In God we trust.  Or distrust.
This penny is dangerous.  Minted the year my daughter was lost.
Beware of tube tops, lug-soled boots.  Beware of ear piercing:
the more holes, the more trouble leaks out.
Trouble was the blue hair.  The pink.  The aubergine.
Fashion pages.  Mirrors.  Bikinis.  Dope.
The boy with dreadlocks.  The river guide.  Magic mushrooms.

Lincoln's looking on in profile.  His lips thin as is he.
As thin as she was.  Honest Abe thought I could not tell a lie,
but I did, for when she began to starve herself,
I lost all liberty, all God-trust. There was no God.
In 1981, nothing was real but her skeletal hands
and coppery metallic breath upon my neck.  Each night, in secret,
I poured out liters of saccharined diet drink
and refilled them with sugared Sprite to bring her –
my hardest, brightest, thinnest penny – back alive.

## *Zodiacal Glow*

She wakes at the beach to night-creak of cottage
in wind, to surf-sounds rough as fraying cloth,

stridulation of insects. In the late moonrise,
her shoes, like Emily's, overflow with pearl.

Her mind untethered by midsummer's eve,
she considers solar dust and how astronomers

plot unexplained starlight.
In a double-exposure of now and then,

a pig-tailed girl sits cross-legged on floorboards,
playing jacks in the half-tones, unconcerned

about star seeds and zodiacal glow. Twosies,
threesies, foursies in rhythmic order, not yet alert

to the spot where the window meets the wall,
the universe expands, and things begin to fly apart.

## Getting Tattooed the Hard Way

After the surgery where they took the breast tissue
and the nipple, after they twisted a back muscle
across my chest, grafted skin for an areola,
they cut a fishtail, used
a purse-string stitch to form a small bud.

This they tattooed into a lovely pink rose.
*Pigment and palette: Beige 10, Beige 1, Pink 1, Brown 2.*
A numb rose, artificial on a man-made hill.
*A Rubenesque body, injured Mona Lisa smile.*

The landscape is a dream, benign fields of
tufted cotton where I'm searching
for someone who's lost, a white labyrinth
with a mirror; and when I turn a corner, I'm walking
unclothed into an counterfeit image.

Scar tissue is stronger than flesh yet weaker, too.
*Hedge-clipper hum of needle. Sting of punctured flesh.*
There's the rosebud, but how can I tender it?
*A Rubenesque body, angry Mona Lisa smile.*

## *Let Me Tell You About the Rat-Zapper*

You tell the children all cancers are not the same.
Your friend is dying, but you are not:
your cells held in check while hers multiply.
This is, of course, one more Rat-Zapper lie.

If you buy it (the man on the radio promises)
for the basement or garage, the rats will be
driven mad by electric shocks and will flee
as they did from Hamelin. But this won't happen.
At 2 A.M., they'll scrabble through the walls
in crazed circles, gnawing wire and insulation,
tangling their pink, hairless tails. Then pulling
in opposite directions, they'll die there,
and the smell will rise upward
to foul your bedroom and your dreams.

No lemon-drop day will sweeten this night-scourge.
Instead of scuttling rats' feet, silence.
But multiplication continues, so retreat is temporary
with a money-back guarantee of more lies to come.

## *Immortality of Culture*

In the dream, I was wheezing as if shrink-wrapped
and wild to fill my lungs with air.
A daytime dream staccato with ravens
in branches of winter trees,
their cries tearing holes
in the thin blue fabric of the sky.

In the photos, my friend is in China
with cormorants, India with a live boa,
and there's a revolving door
and her voice mouthing my name,
yet when I awaken, only the ravens are there.

*Do you ever have that feeling,* a child asked me, *where
the truth is coming, but you don't want to know the truth?*
Or the inevitability, I tell myself, like sailors know a storm
is close when all their knots have drawn tight.

O, the brain is tightly-grooved, its mysteries
found only after death.
But ravens are crying. Earth is spinning,
and cells in Petri dishes
keep replicating – immortality
of culture. No code. The spin is

accelerating toward the speed
of light. Looking out, I see a woman falling
before she falls, with no way
to change the past. In my dream, I struggled
for breath and ravens cried,
and I told the child I saw my friend falling

before she fell and did not, did not
want to examine the knots or know about truth.

## *Fallen Light*

The mile-long breakers threaded north-south
thump against the western shore.

An afternoon of little wind and the shook foil
of water is sparked by a thousand fallen suns.

In their brilliance, I try to measure December's
failing days, anxious to hold them and seine

agates, shells, ancient sand dollar fossils
roiling invisibly below the surf.

Never assume, I remind myself kneeling on iceplant,
because all beauty is promised to darkness

as quartz and granite are ground to sand,
so a life erodes beneath breakers and fallen light;

yet, when the sun is low, even a single grain of sand
casts an angular, heart-stopping shadow.

# II.
# *Lady in the Cube*

## *Eye of the Water Lily*

Night is approaching. The air scented
and pollened yellow.
Edges are indistinct.
Surrounded by an O'Keefe blossom
with fierce stamens, dappled, gnat-freckled,
she's furled by the lily.
There, folded into the rods and cones
of its golden eye,
a spiral of light cushions the air.
No longer restless, she draws up
her knees, idles where
beauty is pure and joy has form.

This is where she was before she began,
in darkness, knees to her chest,
a rounded, rose-nippled girl-seed
not yet desperate for light.
Dreaming of liquid warmth
and gentle hands, knowing only the imprint
of calyx and pistil,
of unrealized petals.
Damp and smooth and unsuspecting.
Not yet impatient
for ripeness, not yet rooting
wildly toward an idea of flower.

## *Baggage*

*I pack my trunk, and in it I put –*
*my China doll, my trading cards, my ice skates...*

a child's game, once played in many languages and now
for real. Since love draws goods and chattel,
today my trunk is heavy. Then black dogs summon
white nights while I long for weightless flight.

Sleepless, I make lists – like Cousin Bertha who has
the longest Life List of any living Midwestern woman.
But my numbered flocks do not fly free.
Days they scritch for seed about my feet.
At night, still active, they chirrup in the Douglas fir,
and as hearts flail against hollow bones
they peel away threads of my flesh.

Oriana Fallaci says she can sit weeks, months, smoking,
drinking coffee, writing as the Berlin Wall falls
and uprisings bloody Tiananmen Square. Oriana has
no trunk, no homing flock with a taste for suet.

*But I pack my trunk and in it I put –*
*their old skates and mittens, their lists and mine.*

## Seeing the Outline

*It's all done with mist and a mirror or two.*
— Leonora Carrington

In the North, people say, if you move quickly
through clouds of mosquitoes,
you can see the outline of where you have been.

I mustn't move with enough speed,
since I see no evidence of myself:
she, that woman in the mirror. Distorted by

sunlight wefted through curtains, she moves
as if submerged in lake water,
unselfconscious but seldom fiercely awake.

There are bears outside, she knows, mostly indifferent,
in the raspberry thicket near the fire lane
while her children's children, keen to steal

their midsummer treat, hover nearby.
As mosquitoes swarm, bears rock on their haunches,
lips inhaling berries, teeth tinted pink.

The woman – focused two generations back
yet two forward – leaves the mirror, then the cabin.
With little idea of where she's been,

she must confront children and bears.
Unsubmerging, displacing mosquito-whine,
she becomes me again, but I am still hesitant,

too slow, seeing mirrors and mist but no outline.

## Lady in the Cube

Center ring: the sideshow is back
but no more dog-faced boys, hermaphrodites,
or wild men of Borneo shown in a tent
for an extra 50 cents.

Now, it's the Python Prince,
Or Vesuvius the Human Volcano
and Mysticlese climbing sabers
then walking on crushed glass.

But the star is Marina, the Lady in the Cube.
Once, she was courted by a man
who dreamed of a beauty he could lock in a cube,
and she told him to get lost,
yet didn't admit
how she loses herself
while bent in a 14-inch coffin of glass.
Vanishes and sees:
the flight of a bird,
a camel ride through desert dunes,
or a woman alone, stretching her legs
as she sips hot, black coffee.

Through the prism of the sideshow, an exaltation,
a place eccentrics live without shame,
where the heart quickens,
where a woman in a cube can unbend and escape.

## *Vermeer's Wife / Vermeer*

Always in debt and he'll never make
anything of himself, Mother says.
Then borrow more from her and others,
get buns on credit while I mind ten babes
and, in his studio, the Master paints,
tasting silence and the perfect woman.

I was that girl and unsplintered woman
with the curls, calm, reading by a window,
no diapers or unpressed clothes.
No fishwife-voice lashing at children
for tracking mud.  No bloated belly
or lye-cracked hands.  No megrims or bills.

His paintings of those women?  Are they of use?
Well, the baker took one for bread.
Though we've moved in with Mother now,
he cares only for light and props.
My pearl earrings and distressed Sunday skirt?
Props like me to be used and reused.

With his camera obscura, he relishes
women in light, but I'm the dark-beneath
and still as the women he paints.
Soon, I'll offer the baker another picture.
The butcher, too.  And soon, we'll have
yet another shadowed, unstill mouth to feed.

*Repose, mouth unmoving,*
*bathed in light.*
*Her dresses, her mother's –*
*the blue or yellow*
*rimmed in fur. Looking out, away,*
*possessed of a secret life,*

*the still-hope of the young.*
*A letter, a fan, a lute,*
*the slanted gaze.*
*A frieze of splendid isolation:*
*woman on the cusp. Becoming.*
*Face in a mirror.*

*That instant before*
*she or the fruit in the bowl*
*begins to rot.*
*Yellow paint, yellow glaze.*
*Sheered pigment,*
*veils of enamel clarity,*

*those polished patches*
*of abstraction.*
*Unflawed.*
*The chaste surfaces.*
*Restraint and consummation*
*overlaid.*

## *Louise Nevelson: Architect of Shadows*

A mysterious world where blackness swallows
light.  Many questions, few replies.
This place feels safe yet, still, heavy with danger.

Crates, boxes sculpted into a cathedral of wood.
Chair legs, slats, staves, shutters.  Drawers
that won't open.  A spiral with no beginning or end.

As a child, Louise culled oddities
from her father's junkyard.  The rest of her life,
she puzzled lost pieces, bonded them with

hammer and nails.  A hand with three fingers.
Circle and arc, pegs of a violin, a cone, a cube,
bowling pins, wheels, molding of leaves and grapes.

Precarious, off-balance planes lend shadows
to the shadows.  Into each box Louise
put a secret, watched the dark embrace it.

What hides, you ask, behind slats and staves?
Why, the debris of the mind, complex and reaching
cathedral-like toward an idea of sky.

So, conceal your secrets in your own deep boxes
offering shade and shelter until all
that's visible is black, black, black, black, black.

# *Gertrude Stein and* Picasso: *On Picasso*

a creator who creates
to complicate things in a new way
possessed by the necessity
of emptying himself
and the appearance and always the appearance

*all the tricks of the intellectual charlatan*

paintings have that strange quality
of an earth that one has never seen
in blues, roses, monotones
the lines of the body harder
and the spirit of everybody changed

*today ... no consolation and exaltation from art*

Cubism, the beauty of realisation
and of things destroyed as they have
never been destroyed
acrobats, clowns, large women
darkness, the beauty of fecundity

*only the peculiar, the eccentric, the scandalous*

not the simple solutions of Braque
but a melange
features seen separately
destroy the rest, as everything
in the 20th century destroys itself

*and celebrity means sales, consequent affluence*

his vision: to make things evolve as they
did not evolve
to express the things we do not see –
ferocity in many dimensions
the long struggle, the splendor

*me? no, I am only a public clown, a mountebank*

## The Tarot Fool Steps Into Space

Conventional wisdom says the Fool is male,
but – poised on a promontory ringed
by jagged peaks of ice – she mirrors me,
her knee-length dress, sleeves like dove's wings
riffling with yellow hair in a silent wind.
Feather in her cap and rucksack on a pole,
she waves a white rose in one hand, gazes
beyond white sun into yellow sky, her long legs
and yellow boots keen to dance past the edge.
A manic ghost of a dog, gaze aligned
with hers, jigs at her heels, haunts the margins
of her world.  And suspended in the air above:
a mysterious letter O, a benediction
in sunlight that haloes an unrepentant head.

## *Purple Echoes*

After the break, the weatherman said, he'd talk
about purple echoes: tornadoes careening through
the south, leveling cities and farms as well as
trailer parks. When they struck, cows floated
Chagall-like on air with cars, rooftops, baby beds.
Showers of shattered glass rained from the sky.
Godzilla, an 8-foot lizard, escaped from his cage,
and nearby, a monkey was eating stray cats.

A stillness in the eye. Though not transported to Oz,
she was floating, too. Weightless for a moment,
buffeted by her own purple echoes: severed poppies
brushing her cheeks, the meadow scented by
wild azaleas where she knelt on a white rock
by the stream, winged dryad lithe and unironic,
pre-Raphaelite hair bright on her back and shoulders.
Before the storm. Before the end.

In the science museum, the tornado surges and forms
in its Plexiglas cylinder, clear image braiding upwards
against gray-black walls. No lizards or monkeys
or showers of sharp glass. No ache from the perfume
of white azaleas. Instead, something contained
and controllable. Something halted with the flick
of a hand or allowed to rise.
Beauty but no echoes. And no hint of purple.

## *Michael Mazur: Ice Glen, 1993*

Interior landscape and the cryptic world of nature,
branching inward with grace.

White arteries and deep-carved black veins,
cave of the body with the heart not visible.

Instead ice-chinked cracks and fissures of stone,
amalgam of art and space.

Left behind: tortured lilies and foliage,
carnivorous plants with their swatches of color,

layers of glaze. Now, old meanings, new techniques –
the painter views his own sudden heartwork,

images of bright and dark blood leaking
through capillaries, a drenched, linear frieze

cold yet temperate, altered from five senses
to relay only sight,

two dimensions, flattened and drained of tint.
In this tangled space, a compaction:

the body's mental garden, roots pulsing out
and down past arbitrary borders of canvas and flesh.

## *Archaeology of Falling*

there's nothing to prove  she begins
this is not a competition you have to win

*in the ancient cistern in Istanbul*

it's an exploration  she continues
a landscape of foreign complexities
of the unexamined

*Medusa  her proud head and neck – a column*

all I ask is two things  she whispers
as over and over the possibilities replay themselves

*snake hair  wide eyes green with time*

no lies and unconditional love
he's listening yet laughing  pursuing archaeology
the unexamined vessel  the hidden smile

*stone-face turned herself to stone*

a delicate probe  she murmurs  chance
and the deceit of darkness and light

*underwater  submerged upside-down  smiling*

and afterwards she says  there is
no afterwards  new territory  old loss
leave the stone unturned

*visible  yes  but still forever  a lie and a loss*

## *Illumination*

Worrying an illuminated manuscript, you sit alone
in your cell with pen, ink, and fine sand.

On the other side of the mirror, a woman on a bed
fingers leaves one by one.

At first, close to drowning:
a time of breakers and nightingale cries,
and you could speak of this to no one.

How you split the sky with a silver arrow.
How, on her palm, you drew yourself,

jester with a dark wand and torn doublets,
visible until the layered fool was made faint by kisses.

A manuscript, the monks said, must sing and fly,
translucent so the written echoes the unwritten.

An ink-blotted ache toward stillness,
breakers reflected in glass, journey over water,

then unroll the parchment.
Listen to the notes the nightingale does not sing.

Now beyond reach, the woman in the glass
is climbing a mountain,

her back to the sea, her feet curious,
the tune she hums jagged as the trail.

You want her story, her song, her body supine
in your bed, your wand by her side,
her hands piecing your tattered costume.

Restless for words and color, you conjure her.
Since she has climbed the mountain, you need not.

Your pen scratches.  Her needle pricks.
The dark nightingale has remembered his old song.

# Self-Portrait in Ink

*in the beginning  there was the line  a straight one or*
        a pen  paper  freedom   don't ask where I've been
*a curved line   always an elegant solution*
        where I'm going   it's a fun house with mirrors
*not volume  not color but line*
        and dark tunnels  dim lights burning red
*a serpent  a mark  a shadowed visibility*
        see the shadows dance across the wall
*shading is only an echo of line  a whisper*
        spiraling shadow of the shadows
*a stand-in for the real   if the line curves*
        quiet yet turbulent teeming with words  syllables
*bone or skin   flower or fruit*
        cacophony of strange music for ears and eyes
*fingers  arms  legs  breasts*
        this afternoon I dreamed my ear was severed
*how can this be*
        a new one glued on in its place
*a pulsating world explaining everything yet*
        was I at the brink of madness
*nothing    on paper  on canvas  on tile*
        or was I only a haunted artist  musician  poet
*only essence   between night and morning*
        seeking not mutilation but a better organ
*death  life are the hollow volumes*
        look  I'm the outsider  classic outsider
*insubstantial  and hard to control*
        I can't  I won't do it  be there  whatever

*weightless   still they cut across*
      when I walk into a room  I'm drawn to
*whiteness   and something*
      the flashing red sign that says EXIT
*materializes   a dimensional presence*
      when I sit by a fire or walk a mountain path
*a darkening crosshatch of memory*
      I like to be alone   move at my own pace
*and I smell fermented berries*
      engaged in some interior monologue
*blackberries staining the nibs of my pen    I taste them*
      aware my public and private selves are enemies
*feel the seeds between my teeth*
      and if I mix them together
*feel the crackle*
      yes  I fear  there might be blood
*taste the ink  as it bleeds black on my tongue*

## Rotation to Winter

Red is mostly gone, but faded yellow
maples the air, spirals in the wind,
stars the wet ground.

Wind-messages fan from the north.
Clouds surge until I can feel
the earth's rotation to winter,
and sun behind clouds
masquerades as a cold evening
moon.

Having left this place as a girl,
I return as to a foreign land,
surprised to find
there is
one last rose of summer

bright amid the rusting brown.
But now this is an alien place.
I have no coat to stop the wind, no
way to keep the rose.

## *From the Wing Bone of a Crane*

Anemophiles, lovers of wind, believe time
is infinite, and the past has no claim,

but in China there's a 9,000 year old flute
carved from the wing bone of a crane.

Once, at Jiahu in the Yellow River Valley,
flood and ebb, rice ribboned green, and crane

on one leg in the shallows, his target-red eye
scanning fish.  A rock flies.  Feathered death.

O solemn bone, white and hollow and smooth.
Seven chiseled holes, a delicate windy sound,

millennium after millennium lost
only to be unearthed, brown and mottled,

trilled again by other lips and fingers.
Same flute.  Different song.

The human brain weighs little and is lightly
grooved, yet it knows when a flute is a flute.

Anemophiles might embrace this bone.
Or say it does not, cannot possibly exist.

# The Rest of the Landscape is Dim, Pleading Ignorance

Trees dead and dying mirrored in water.
Triangle of uneasy trunks. Needles feather
the ends of dry branches. Nest-splinters propped
in the black tree and bobbed over the blue lake.

This is a painted world
where foreground steeps into middle distance.
Beyond blue, light scrims and periwinkles.
Between here and there in the unseen air

they are walking a blue trail, silent feet
and mouths, pushing their dead before them
or drawing them behind. Blue air and wind
pleat them with those who lead and follow.

Someone else is there. A girl-child, her bluish hair
uncombed, her face prim and guarded.
But she is braver than she looks. Soprano tones
ripple from her, rising to pink and purple the air.

# III.

# *Blue Roses*

## *Bright Princess: Moment of Impact*

There's the speed and the brightness of glass.
God, how I love that word *bright*.
Fine French wine is surging mid-summer
through my dark veins,
but I'm tired – so tired I've asked my girl
to drive the Grande Corniche.  She's only 14, you see,
but already clever behind the wheel.
And mid-day sleep is luscious
mingled with tannin on the tongue as I angle
in back, collage myself into all the princesses
I've ever been.  Satin, velvet, sable.
Meissen.  Burma jade.  Crepe de Chine.  Then there's
an odd lurch, a spin,
and cliffs of brightness break against my crown.

## *Kursk Good-Bye*

Nadia, my cabbage, don't think of me here in the underworld
without you.  Think of the Chagall print over our bed
with its bride and groom and wild-eyed blue cow.

Yes, love, your worst nightmares have become real.
Our submarine at the bottom of the Barents Sea.
Explosions, fire, flooding – only a handful still alive.
Emergency lights are dimming.  Soon they'll fail.
We're short on oxygen, leaking.
Here in the ninth compartment, many are injured,
others weeping and clutching one another.
Vlady has soiled himself.  Dmitri is writing a poem.
We've no way to surface, so there will be no escape.

And me?  I'm here yet not here, listening for chords of
that symphony you like – Rachmaninoff, maybe,
where bells ring out at the end.  Music might make me
forget your grandmother's featherbeds,
berries we'll never pick, latchkeys we will not lose,
children who won't know "Eyewinker" and "Chinchopper."
Oh, Nadia, we never got to Petersburg or Istanbul.
We never tasted artichoke or caviar,
never caught fireflies or rode a toboggan,
but enchanted by Chagall, we laughed,
and, freed from laws of gravity and common sense,
we held hands, rose up and saw our town, its pathways,
its chicks and chickens, as we floated above rooftops.
Together we were weightless, loving ourselves
and each other inside our paperweight world.

A world too young to turn real.  Too new for you to carp
about mildewed clothes, how I chewed food,
how you felt when I took you from behind.  No ridicule
for the uselessness of the skinny egret I whittled
from the handle of a mop; but Nadia, the lights are
hissing.  It's, at the same time, hot and cold.  More water.
Now the lights are out.  Ivan has a torch, but I
am writing blindly, touching myself with my left hand,
thinking of you.  Pretend I am not under water
but on a black raft, afloat on an endless tropical sea
with black breakers and black palms waving overhead,
and you're here.  It's your hand, your mouth
I feel in this obscene darkness.  Yes – but wait –
look – the black sky is lightening, and I hear bells,
all the bells of Russia are ringing
and ringing out at once, and we are not, after all,
on a raft but on the back of a wild-eyed blue cow,
cantering across the arc of night sky

as dandelions of light burst  before our eyes,
and the bells, they are vibrating, shaking, shaking
us both, and, Nadia, Nadia – do you hear them?  Do you –

## Mary Todd Lincoln at Ford's Theatre

So I said no, no more dramas like these with pieces of my flesh
being peeled away by birds of prey, and, still, I put on
the black-and-white striped silk and settled black lace on my head,
but other than that
it was a night like many with the walls closing in on me
and sound of rat tails in the walls and spiders and roaches
streaming over inked velvet, and so I said *Stop and Let it stop now*,
because I have exhausted my strength for others' freedom –
you see, I was a Southern girl raised right, though morbidly,
and did what my father said and was gracious to the dark-skinned,
met their eyes and gave them their due,
for a good Christian soul should not shirk but give all good measure,
and so I gave and give to them now, give to the President who owns my life
and my sons (though the Lord took two back) and to the world, too,
letting everyone enter to pick at strips of tender skin,
but other than that
what has it gotten me but here and here and here, play within a play,
into this dark box where I sit holding the President's hand,
corseted, constricted by time and chance, my hair tight-pinned
under its grieving-Madonna drape while my head swells
and I feel stings as hordes of bees begin to siphon honey
from my eyes and ears, from my breasts and beneath my skirts,
and though I should be grateful and say blessed be the sinners,
blessed be those who hear the call of duty,
blessed be the free hearts of those with skin black as coal,

but other than that
if there were a way to stop my life now I would – no, I do not lie,
and I would, if I had my father's Derringer and a bullet here,
put a stop to the shrinking walls and birds of prey,
to rats and roaches, spiders and bees, to the vanishing skin,
and I'd draw a Kentucky bead and *Bang* I'd say,
because as every Christian is capable of love, so is he capable
of murder as am I, and I'd put an end to this suffering
but other than that
why shouldn't it be now before I am stripped to sinew and bone,
before it is only my bones that can dance, only bones of fingers
left to grasp the President's own, and then there will be
no more tired endurance at this interminable play and my role will
be unlearned and undone because what I say will not be
long-remembered, and it can, if I act, stop
in an hour, in a scene, in a minute, in a heartbeat...
but other than that
now that they, the other dark ones, have been freed,
let me, too, be freed from myself and from this killing darkness – *Bang.*

## Adolf's Mother Imagines the Future

In the loose pollen of her daydreams,
this son of hers shone and she sang to him,
taught him to stand straight and tall.
When she washed him, she scrubbed
to peel the Schicklgruber taint
and leave him pure and white beneath.
His privates, too, she soaped
with care, so he would not carry the stink
of common humanity. That touching,
she told him smacking his buttocks,
was all right yet he mustn't touch himself.

He wasn't, alas, the blue-eyed flower of
her dreams: a blonde girl with
ribboned plaits, but he had a curious mind.
For hours, he'd gaze at his face
in the bowl of a spoon, turning himself
fat or thin or upside-down. Or at his profile
shadowed on a wall. Even the way he
teased wings off a honeybee or dissected
the half-dead mice the cat brought home
showed his special bent.

And, afterwards, he was a good boy. Always
let her help him wash off his hands
and brush under his nails. Filth, she taught,
striking him only when necessary,
is everywhere. A person can't be too careful.
In the milkweed silk of their days,
she cherished her son. Then when she lay
with him in the dark, she saw him ringed by
pinwheels of light, marching
smart and sure-stepped into morning,
singing a song and waving his clean hands.

## *Holocaust Museum: Crematorium II*

A scale model sculpted from plaster: that's all it is. So why does it have such power? Hundreds of tiny figures walk, move, lie within a pristine world, ice-white like timeless friezes from the pediment of the Parthenon.

Undressing:
hats coats gloves scarves
dresses jackets shirts
shoes stockings panties
watches rings lockets

white-faced with shame, they cry white
tears  remove layers of chalky clothes
cover themselves with thin white towels
and hands  avert white, frightened eyes

Gassing:
lock the door  bar it
check through peepholes
Zyklon B: prussic acid
pellets drop kill
some gone in an instant
all in 20 minutes
then pump in fresh air

here they howl their silent white screams
clutch the albino bodies of their children
stare in dull-white horror at showerheads
step on whited bodies of the fallen
swim through a tide of white death  and
with colorless lips rimming black-holes
struggle toward the white brink of Lethe

Cremation:
shave women's heads
pull gold teeth
check body orifices for
hidden valuables
nothing human left
3 or 4 to an oven depending
upon size
only 1000 a day
a waste when they could gas
7 times that

white stretchers carried by white guards
white cordwood-stiff bodies to be pillaged
white-faced, white-shouldered Jews shove
whitened bodies of the dead into white ovens
while grim white-starched guards oversee
white world still and bloodless where
white men sought whiteness  and now we need
white to purge the evil just white all over
white white nothingness only white white
white white white white white white white...

51

## *Einstein's Daughter*

In 1914, steeped in Brownian motion,
photoelectrics,
the marked irregularity
of Mercury's orbit around the sun,

Einstein wrote his wife Mileva,
mother of his sons, asking her to:
(1) keep his linen in order,
(2) serve him 3 meals a day in his room,
(3) address him only when required.

When he met Mileva, an ethnic Serb,
she was a physics student, too,
and he called her his dollie
who made his pillow catch fire.

Their love-child Lieserl –
given away the year
before they married – vanished.
But what was she like?

Did she hear music of spheres?
Or did she tend meals and linen,
then board a Dachau train
with her children
knowing only that
relativity is what happens to you?

## *The Girl Who Flew Like a Kite*

The girl, who wanted to subtract herself from
a terror of voices, rose up tethered only

by twine from her dragon kite, ten fingers
coiled in the grooves of its red plastic handle

as its patchwork tail, a translucence, luffed,
triangulating her skin to sheets of stained glass.

Overhead, the dragon crackled, tail taut, air
cooling, the girl's eye fixed on eye of the dragon.

*Don't drop me,* she whispered as sky became
home, as wind blew comfortably chill,

numbing mother-father voices pursuing
her and each other into static silence.

Below her now, a snowscape, the earth's maze
disappeared, all things large spun small

and harmless so even a child could control them.
Her nails were growing, her neck lengthening

as she skimmed from blue into white
and back into blue.  Strong and long, safe now,

her face rapt with ice crystals
in this still place where she could breathe freely

as she and the other dragons, exhaling
delicate petals of flame, ruled the skies.

## *Breaking Away From the Family*

I'm there. See me in yellow? Not the short one
with no visible arms. That's my sister.
I'm the frowning-smiling girl eyeing the family.
See us? Sister, Sister, Mother, Baby. Then Brother,
at his board-like best, standing in too-big overalls
trying to be Papa. We're caught there,
nailed and glued to a door with no house,
a door that won't open. Only my half-laced
boots are real. The rest: flat-tinted,
an odd two dimensional, one-handed girl.

The part of me that's broken away
has grown tall, drives a car, goes to work, lives
in a house with a real door. She's warm
and full-fleshed and dances with boys under
a flower moon. But the splintered girl I was
keeps coming back, returns me here
to stare at Mother's pork sausage fingers,
at her dress with its bear-claw flowers.
Overhead, black scrolls hold her and them
like curved iron bars of a jail insisting:

You may never leave
or change or be part of any family
except this one staring helplessly outward.
Papa will not return.
Brother will not become Papa.
Baby will always be propped in Mother's lap.
Sister will never find her arms.
The five of us will always be
the last picture Papa saw before he went,
a stiff wooden portrait left behind.

## Blue Roses in Angria

      Charlotte Bronte's gloves, a pair of French leather ones, impossibly tiny, have ended up in a display case at Haworth, and though I should be obsessed by the fact that the fingers that once rested in these gloves created little Jane Eyre and Mr. Rochester with his mad wife Bertha, all I can think of is the childhood days Charlotte shared with her four sisters, Maria, Elizabeth, Anne, Emily, and her brother Branwell and of their enchanting worlds of Angria and Gondal, before she had the harsh reality of losing her siblings to tuberculosis, opium, and alcohol,

                          yet she carried on, wrote books, stood in front of the cheval glass to put on her neat straw bonnet and little gloves (oh, the vanity of the plain woman) before she went to London to visit her publisher trying to look as if her rough hands hadn't spent much too much time darning socks, peeling potatoes, emptying chamberpots, washing dirty linen, bloody handkerchiefs, and menstrual rags.

      Then, suddenly, the misty cheval glass clears and I see she wasn't reviewing her royalties at Smith, Elder & Co. but unclasping those leather-gloved fingers from her bosom so she could slip in the side door of a Chelsea townhouse, drop her bonnet and cape to the floor, loosen coiled hair, as her lover used his lips to peel off the gloves finger by finger before he seized her in his arms, in a blizzard of petticoats, whisking her to the land of Angria with its blue rose petals, to Angria, where light honeycombed through the trees and dolphins breached in the waves while in the air – butterflies, gentle spirits of the unborn, and then,

                          in the heat of passion, he seized those French gloves murmuring and murmuring, taking them, pressing one of them into service, using it to fend off the babies' souls, feeling bliss yet quite unable to peer into the future and imagine someone might put them in a glass case, might then remove them, test for the DNA inside and discover why sweet Charlotte never, ever wore those tiny gloves again.

## *Death of a Podiatrist*

Please don't laugh.  This is serious.
I was at a play and Arthur Miller, too,
though it wasn't his.  On stage,
there was a cast, solemn and intent,
lines learned, places blocked out,
a grave business, and I thought
it was *House of Mirth,* and that was
Lily Bart up there kicking back her train
with one foot and skirting danger.
Surrounding her were men –
middle-aged and graying – their lives:
old coins, minted, dated, clinking ominously,
but then I was with them
on stage, and Lily Bart was no where
to be seen though I had her purse.
The metallic sound swelled until
I could feel weight, taste copper
on my tongue.  Still, it wasn't me
in danger but a man who looked like
Willy Loman in a morning coat
dying before my eyes.
I knew and loved him, yet all I did was
change costume from white to red,
put the purse on the chair at stage right,
walk through a practiced pattern
that pretended to be real life.
Lights shifted.  Though I was spotlighted,
the man was not.  Checks and balances
changed.  Doorways darkened, and my feet,
in Lily's high-heeled slippers, hurt.
I needed help, but the lines weren't mine.
This was the death of a podiatrist.
A podiatrist?  I don't know why.
But please don't laugh.  This is serious.

## *Escaping Sodom*

Who's at the door?  Him?  He can take me then.
If you are spared and the children, I'll do anything.

But I must pack.  Our marriage rings.  Their lost teeth.
Fresh bread.  Sky before morning.  Dew.  The way

the hummingbird trusts the honeysuckle.
The way you trust me.  Digging for fresh water must

continue and the probe of the midnight skies.
Sweet salt of kisses and the turn of a key in a lock.

Tender passwords need to be remembered, so I am
not locked out.  How to exit.  How to resume

without damage.  New grass, the arc of summer,
the ninth wave, and everything beneath the bed.

Packages of onion and mustard seed, bright poppies
not yet exploded into possibility.  More knocking.

Now what?  Is there an arbitrary time limit?  Then
hurry.  Take them and their promise in your arms.

Bundle our memories, and don't wait.  If you're
all out there before me, I might not need to turn back.

## In a Jail of My Own

Now summer has come to the mountains,
And yellow henbane blooms.
Clay walls weep, the door's ajar,
Khamsin blows through windows.
Last night, my heart in chains,
I made love to your old blue shirt
Smelling of onions,
Of sweet carnation and smoke.
Through your stone wall, did you hear me cry out?

## The Magician's Apprentice

Done with mirrored boxes or silk scarves,
so when I leave, for him, I cease to exist.
Later, he'll wave a want or a wand, conjure me,

and – until the world clamors –
I'll be his dark matter, his sleight-of-hand,

as he reaches out, plucks me again,
says I am his love,
his center, his sudden pearl from the sea

when in truth, I am no more than
his pupil, sometime favorite, occasional trick.

# Marilyn M. Thinks About French & Russian Dogs

*Du Chien*
a French phrase (that can't really be translated) –
used to describe Tolstoy's wife
and sometimes me, since I want
to be a Tolstoy heroine –
is supposed to be about sexiness:
*avoir d'élégance, de la séduction.*
But I think, after all,
it's only another way of pointing out

who a man might tame
or teach to fetch
one who can learn on command
come, sit, stay, lie down, shake hands
someone to pet but one happy
with bones tossed in her direction
and she'll follow his lead
play dumb, play dead
walk by his side, get the paper
accept scraps, beg for treats, for affection
lick him with her rough pink tongue
invite him to enter from behind
warm his bed, stay home
waiting for him to reappear
obey, fetch, speak when prompted
know her place
be grateful yet like a wolf
be dangerous
capable of sinking fangs into his throat.

*Du chien* has possibilities, I think,
but it does when used by a man
still mean *doggy* and, also, *bitch*...

## *Paramedics at the Scene of the Dog Mauling*

Oh, we see people dying, people dead yet never this.
Remember the scene in *The Shining* – yes, Jack Nicholson –
where blood seeps down the hallway, then rises, flows
into a river? Well, as a flood like this is receding,
we get to the apartment and something that was a woman
is lying there in the terrible red sea of a corridor,
her clothes torn to patches and her flesh, too.
The scene? An abattoir like we saw once in Paris with
the same sick, iron-stench of blood. Hysteria is there, too,
wearing crimson, red lips shining as she licks at them,
red lips gaping as she screams her Munch screams,
cries with no weight or volume. Her eyes are red also,
and she's pulling up her dress, offering us the red
between her legs, a wild threat, a dare. We see
people shouting, keening, but we have been stricken,
have no hearing, no voice, no more sense of smell,
feel only slippage of the vile red-black carpet,
slick of the fresh-tinted blood-red walls. *The dogs?* you ask.
*Dogs of Hades.* Gone now yet echoes of their cries
rock us backwards, knock us down until we are
sliding, being swallowed by a place beyond the real.
Still, yes, we have the gloves, the body bag,
and a puzzle of kidneys, colon, liver, ribs, skin.
Listen, I can't keep talking about this.
Anyone who tries to describe the dead-white
of living bone when it's first exposed to air and light
will fail. Anyone who sings about love
and the glories of the flesh has never stood
where we now stand. And all the while Hysteria

is smiling at us, chucking us under our chins
and then, as we gape, sucking the tip of a length
of sinew, using it to thread her bone needle,
because she's going to make us a bright new quilt.
But – wait, no... stop – that's no quilt but a shroud,
and we feel it here around us
drawing tighter, shrink-wrapping us, hot and viscous,
impossible to shuck.  Wrapped inside with us: bone,
teeth, gristle but nothing human left.  No shining
moments.  Not even a scream.  Only the echo of a scream.

## *Janis Says:* Burn, Baby, Burn

Stars splash from the wake of a steep blue sky
And stripes furrow flesh scored with blood
Stars orbit the full moons of my ass
And stripes jack the twin suns of my tits
Stars trail barbs of light through fields of weed
Stripes bleed like acid-pricked skin
Stars forfeit their edges one by one
Stripes flay themselves into raveling nooses
Stars  round and wide-eyed now  boom the music of the spheres.

In the rockets' red glare I pledge allegiance to the flag
And to myself and long may we wave
My country wrong or wrong   God damn America
He's not *my* Uncle Sam
The rain which should be cold is scalding me
In amber waves  flame sucks flame

As flames spark from eyes and mouth
They splash  orbit  trail  forfeit  boom
They furrow  jack  bleed  flay  scorch
Melting stars  melding stripes  fusing sky and earth and flesh
Because I'm hot  so combustibly hot

*Burn and let the swords melt to ploughshares*
*And let stripes sweep from sea to fucking sea*
*And let stars smoke upwards into twisted galaxies*

Is anybody listening

*We have bared our souls and our bodies*
*So we can dip ourselves in this fresh fire*
*So we can sing God Bless America*
*Sing O say can you see and rest here when day is done*

## You, Walking Out of the Ashes

A gray specter, you're picking your way out of the ashes
and asking me to dance. (Why is the metaphor always dance?)

My skirt is singed, heavy with smoke and my hair soot-black,
but I reach out, taking the ash-silvered rose from your hand,

clenching it between my teeth so I can angle my body
close to yours while we glide one more tango.

Our steps – *slow, quick-quick, slow* – are muffled by cinders,
yet we're brazen and others, shamed by our filth, avert their eyes.

Was it only this morning I fed dogs, pruned roses, pulling
away from you, from your Brioni suit and the diamond choke-chain

anchored around my neck? *Beware,* Grimm tales always say,
*of what you wish for.* Well, today my third wish

(my worst wish) came true. And, still, I ask you one more time:
go back to Monday, forget your briefcase, slip your necktie-noose

and dance with me here before towers of light, hold me against
your two-beat heart before the world catches fire,

(Why has the metaphor become fire?) before the surreal
turns real and before your fingerbones beckon.

# IV.
## *Fire Is Favorable*

## *Putting Your Money Where Your Mouth Is*

You've been traveling a lot, my love.
That's why when you telephone,
all I can ever hear is the clink of shekels,
rustle of rands, the weight of pounds.

When you come back home and kiss me,
I can taste the acrid metal of lira and pesos,
feel marks across my teeth and the oil
of drachmas coating my tongue

At night in bed, you cover me with yen,
guilders, shillings, euros, farthings,
array my breasts with riyals, kroner, francs.
and fill me with mounds of brass pennies.

But, my treasure, the coin of the realm
has proved counterfeit, so I will burn the bills,
melt down loose change to create
an idol you can fondle instead of me.

# Definitions of Twilight

## Civil Twilight: The Engineer

The man who had not invited me to his 70th told me the party had been small, said his young wife kept him young and his new Japanese car could outgun anyone at zero to 60, said he didn't like to think about his quadruple bypass, wasn't sure he wanted to be a grandfather, and that it was odd to be retired yet see his wife go to her office. Because the world had grown darker, he told me, and because street lights seemed too dim at night, he was finally ready to admit to being middle-aged.

## Nautical Twilight: The Agent

The man in the lavender plaid shirt and purple tie said he still had his boat and did anybody want to buy a boat, said he no longer swabbed the deck or polished the brass, admitted his wife would rather go for sushi and to a movie and that he traveled too much and there were too many hotshots on the bay, and the weather was cold, and it was hard to find someone to crew. He told me he hadn't sailed in 6 months but to sell would be to admit horizons were disappearing and that he and the world had changed.

## Astronomical Twilight: The Stargazer

Leaving the men behind, I opened the door and stepped out. In the night sky, a lemon-slice moon and Venus. Then Jupiter with icy Ganymede. Staring, I considered another Ganymede, the beautiful bad boy of Greek myths. In our local myths, the purple-tied man and the one with the young wife had both been beautiful bad boys. Considering the two of them, I waited until the faintest stars were visible, aware I preferred bad boys to men who reserved their passion for fast cars or boats that never left port.

## *What You Want Really Want, Lady:*

Sometimes a cigar is just a cigar and what you want is a bad boy, someone who will take risks, be vulnerable, hopelessly romantic, write odes, someone who will walk on the dark side of the street, who will spend money he doesn't have, who loves his mother best; and, if you're lucky, he'll love you almost as much as he loves his mother, his daughter, his first wife 30 years after he divorced her; and this same boy will appear in your dreams, kneeling on a white sand beach, running his rusty Tonka truck back and forth as he tells you, "You must pay attention." Any good bad boy will lie, cheat, and steal gaudy dimestore rings or cigarettes or a cigar, and he'll get sick smoking behind the garage, and he'll give the rings as promiscuously as smiles to every girl in sight, a Georgie Porgy who kisses the girls and makes them cry – oh, the crying part you can do without, still, it will be worth it because of those kisses, since no one can kiss like a bad boy – the deep kiss that promises everything – rapture and endless love and no lies even if after the rapture it's all smoke and mirrors and transience; but, listen, no bad boy wishes to marry, wear a tie, a wedding band, or wants to own a money clip. He's all *carpe diem*, wants it all now and will take you along for the ride and for the brass ring. Of course, the ring is always brass, though when he slips it on you, it seems to glow with the magic of gold, and you'll say, *yes more, yes, now... fuck tomorrow,* because tomorrow's a shadow over the horizon, and today is cuddling close to him on the woodpile behind the garage with bright dimestore rings adorning your fingers and toes while he offers pudding and pie, tosses his golden curls as he gives you ravishing kisses, before you both lie back, kick up your heels, and smoke a cigar together.

# Letter & Package Bomb Indicators

### 1. Do Not Open

That girl's a walking time bomb. An unstrung package.
Shake her and she rattles. Stamps won't stick.
Her labels are unreliable. Don't peel anything back
or take anything away. Keep her close to home,
packed in cotton. She should have the lightest load,
the shortest route. Let her hold catalogues
and glossy magazines. Don't make her jealous.
Don't ask her what she thinks or how she feels.
Don't weigh her. Don't cancel. Tell her she's perfect.


### 2. Treat As Suspect

Under the sleek exterior of her package lurks
the dynamite of the short-fused child she was.
A pretty brown wrapping will disguise
hazardous materials. Ammunition, too. Spent bullets,
old grenades crammed in with pieces of rope
too short to save, rusted nails, lost bills. Her letters.
They, like her tongue, have always been sharp.
Born in the Year of the Dragon. Handle with care.
Make no sudden moves. This side up. Fragile.
There's no return address. No identifying marks,
so assume the worst. Proceed with caution.

## 3. Call Your Postal Inspector

Meddlers look to the quick fix. A heart-to-heart.
A faceless expert called in to give her the once-over
and shrink-wrap her. Duct tape to contain
volatile and unstable substances. Weigh and measure her.
Assess her destination and the probability she will not
arrive in one piece. Call in a team of experts.
The dogs, too. Let everyone sniff around
and make pronouncements but no decisions.
Delay as long as possible.
Then let someone else make the decision.

## 4. Call The Police

When all else fails, give her up. Let the faceless
and unrelated prod, poke, listen for ominous ticking
or test for explosives. Nothing personal.
Just the facts, ma'am. Did you? Do you? Would you?
Have you ever? You have a right to be silent
even if you never choose silence. Here, the suspicious
will be doubly-suspected. The guilty, guiltier.
The dangerous, totally out-of-control. So they'll leave her
in a field alone. Then they can defuse her
where she can't hurt them or us. A small unavoidable
sacrifice in the name of safety and of peace.

## Burnout Woman & Man of Grass

The burnout gown was meant for her, a film
of cut velvet, low and rounded at the neck,
bias like a Thirties gown draping to cup
breast and ass, show nipple and bush yet conceal
softened flesh on belly and hip and thigh.

The man lay on his back in heat-specked grass,
arching a newspaper above his head
so a sun-mottled shadow, thin as the whisper
of the burnout gown, touched his face,
while his flaccid, unclothed body,

merged to a pointillist surface of flesh
and grass and sky: red, yellow, magenta,
a hundred tints of urgent green.

When the woman shrugged off the gown,
her breast and its azalea scar were visible
as she waited, singing a shallow song of bias
and painted nails and tender flesh.
Still waiting, she eyed the gown, now a cloud

above green carpet, and when the man came,
not through the door but as an outline rising from
a carpet transformed into shagged grass, his skin
was radiant with Seurat's stippled palette.
Though he reached out, it was to lift the pewter cloud.

Cradling it, he began to sing a song of his own,
not to her but to the gown, his voice muffled
as lips crushed its weightless promise.

## *Avalanche Warning*

Sleep is shifting away.  Under the dark cave
of blankets, a man's body by mine.
But it is snowing here.  Yes, in our room, cold flakes
sluice from the high white ceiling.
Unseen crystals crown my head, dissolve
and run down my cheek.  Though motionless,
I am aware of the snow as it continues
to fall.
                       Tasting snow on my tongue,
smelling its metallic freshness, I rise.  Behind me
in bed, the safe silhouette of the sleeping man;
but I am in danger.  Drifts scud at the windows
and door as I remember the Siq at Petra, the banks
of the Zambezi, the eclipse on the Altiplano.
If I stay here, I'll become an ice maiden,
a weightless shadow of white, and there's
some place else I need to be.  By the bed where
the man's rough breath

                       trolls through cold-flaked air,
I strap on crampons, shrug into my pack.
*Wait for me,* I whisper, reaching to twist fingers
in his steel-wool hair.  *But forgive me.*
*For I am not yet done.*  Then peering through goggles
to ward off blindness, I step past swales of
blue-white snow and alone in the dark begin to climb.

# Moving Out

### 1. What Has Happened To Us

Instead of crickets, we wake to mourning
doves, peer through barred windows,
feel sway of wind, grip of fog.
Half our married lives, 33 years spent
on a campus known as The Farm,
then our daughter backed us into
the cage of a city apartment. Everything
costs too much here. Nothing is
the same, and numbers on the digital
clock, even when we stare, seem static.
This week there was an earthquake
we didn't feel; someone we don't
remember sent a phalaenopsis that
needs to be fed orchid food we don't
have; and we saw a new doctor who smiles
with his teeth, who prescribed
new pills that rainbow the breakfast bar.

### 2. What He Does

Thinking about Melville and Hawthorne,
he reshuffles 60 years of academic
papers, cracks at random books he wrote
and ponders what he meant by words
lined across their pages. He uncaps
bottles of pills, watches skin flake and
examines blood bruises under nails.
His daughter has taken away his car,
thinks he doesn't notice. And, before they
moved in, she took off the door chain.
He never saw it, but the uncaulked
holes are there. Holes seem to be

everywhere and wind, too, like this week's
storm named Ishmael. *Call me Ishmael,
because I seem to be at sea and in the brig.*
Why do the grandchildren seem so small, he
wonders, and how has the wind stolen their voices?
Once in Canada (or was it near the House
of Seven Gables) a bear froze
in the beam of his flashlight, staring and
he, curiously unafraid, continued
to advance. Who was he then? Who is he now?
And how will he pay for things?

### 3. What She Does

She waters the orchid and pinches
jaundiced leaves from African violets.
Violets should be happy in the fog,
which doesn't suit her but suits them.
Despite cramps in her knuckles,
she writes the thank-you to
her daughter's friends, plays solitaire.
She can't remember if she took her pills
or the first 50 lines of *Evangeline*.
Boxes of pictures and letters weigh down
the dining room table. Among them,
a letter from Margaret Mitchell,
from when peach blossoms snowed and
before she wrote that book. Then, her
mother wouldn't let her tap or pierce ears
because those things were lower class.
Now, her daughter has become her mother
and is crabby with her. Some days when

she isn't fixed on fire, earthquakes
or hurricanes, she hates her daughter.
Her husband, too, when he stares, like
once in Minnesota when, arcing
his flashlight, he outstared a raccoon.
Last night, she dreamed of snow camping
in Alberta and when doves woke her
decided she'd get a lovebird
but her daughter, who insists they carry
diseases, won't approve. Besides,
even a bird would cost them money.

## 4. What They Each Remember

He: the vanilla of her skin,
how her hair blew across his mouth
as she tugged at his shirt buttons.
She: the taste of hot cornbread when
Anna Mae took it from the oven, how
she lied about her age, because she
was old – 29 – when she married him,
a younger man who thought
she had graceful hands and a sweet voice.
At their house, he liked deadheading
roses and staking soft-furred
tomato vines. She liked to talk, to idle
under wisteria and serve ice tea to
friends or to grandchildren. One of them,
the girl who works downtown in
pin-stripes, is having a baby, and
they'll name it after him, because he's
important. He writes things.

            As sugar to ruby-throats,
he knows, she attracts people.
But does she realize he used to lie about
where he'd been and what took so long?
She never cared about quiet, about
why Melville wrote of the sea, why
Dimmesdale wept.  Now her friends
are dead, his colleagues, too;
and he can't remember what they are
supposed to do with their pills.
She isn't sure if she told him about snow
camping or about the bird.  If she plays
solitaire long enough, he may
go to his room for a nap.  If he rattles
enough paper, she may walk to
the grocery alone.  How will she find
her way back without him there to
guide her?  What will she use for money?

## 5. What We Will Do

Day by day, we save things we are meant
to swallow.  A pair of doves twig
a nest under the eaves.  We write
the Neptune Society.  This is taking too long.
We walk, but it's cold in the fog.
We sleep late, we sleep with TV news
showing accidents of man and nature,
we sleep alone.  We do not touch.
He doesn't listen.  She doesn't listen.
This is taking too long.  Our daughter
lectures us.  The doctor smiles as he lies.

We are so old now, we allow him to lie.
Our voices are rusty from disuse; and we're
waiting for someone to change the paper
in the cage, to take it for recycling. We
need recycling. Once we had one – a cycle
we both could ride on. She was rounder then.
He was taller. Once we fell. She broke her
collarbone. He broke his wrist. It was
his fault. It was her fault. This is taking
too long. The fog makes our bones heavy,
and we can't remember if the deadbolt turns
right or left. Before this, we never had
a deadbolt or this much silence.
The only sound is the hum of the clock.
Everything has a cost. We miss
Princeton, Alberta, Minnesota,
our house. We miss our daughter
who was golden with chestnut curls
and her children whose bodies were
sweaty and golden. Something is crouched
in the shadows. It won't be long now.
He says it's a bear. She knows it's
a raccoon. Still, we can't find our
flashlight, and the shadows keep moving.

## Less Velvet Ropes

the sign said.
Less velvet ropes to fly my satin swing,
less to rock my feather bed,
less to bind my love and hold him.

Pay it out, play it out. That rope is the color of wine,
of old blood, soft to the touch and too easy to sever.

Like Rimbaud, *Je est un autre.* I is someone else,
and to hell with grammar. Rimbaud: like me, stunned by
an abyss of self. But he died young,
while I have become a keeper of string and old roses,
of love notes paid out across bare mountains.
Under closed lids, darkness herringbones,
and time no longer stretches but draws up tight.

In an eyeless corridor, I make my way along velvet ropes
and am afraid. *Less,* the sign said. How much less?

A circular mystery where – despite the dark,
I feel too much is visible. Ropes are short
and frayed here where I am made strange
by ecstasy. Though there is less present, less forever,
I want too much. Tie me and hold me.
Rock the swing and the bed though there's little rope
to hang myself, little to show or to keep.

When Mother reads this, she will shudder,
and he, my love, will smile and sing to me of velvet.

As lovers – held by diminished velvet – we
move like marionettes, spin our own tales,
here alone,
here where distortion is gentle yet not unwitting.

# Fire Is Favorable to the Dreamer

*To Dream of Seeing a Tower Denotes
You Will Aspire to High Elevations*

Perseids firefly the night sky as she launches
herself from the stone turret, curves
through seams of glassy heat and dense shade
toward the Milky Way.  Here, moons of Jupiter
wink like deepwater pearls, and Saturn's rings
splay outward into dust.  All that
defines loses edge until she is no longer
a girl on the cusp.  Desire, wild and weightless,
soaks her.  She shivers and feels its chill,
probing blackness, aware of lust, alert
to rapture.  Then shards of dark diamonds grit
her eyes as a chariot with fiery horses
looms at the horizon, keen to guide her home.

*To Dream Your Slippers Are Much Admired*
*Foretells You Will Be Involved in a Flirtation*
  *That Will Bring Disgrace*

They weren't soft squirrel fur or glass like Cinderella's,
but passionfruit red, and they waltzed her past
mirrors while everyone watched her feet.
Desperate to escape interiors for a life of the flesh,
she found herself butterflied in a meadow
as someone else's love poured wine and fed her berries.
Then exotic sites with strange customs.  White peaks
and dark wells.  Desert dunes, sea-stacks, a gypsy campfire.
Hammocks, lean-tos.  Someone else's love now hers.
Moonlight leaking between trees and starlight from
the edge of time

      until her slippers were worn at the heel,
sole-thinned, warped by rain and mud.
As foolish onlookers eyed them, her mother wailed:
"You play with fire.  Now you're damaged goods
and can't ever come home."

*Fire Is Favorable to the Dreamer*
*If She Doesn't Get Burned*

Cradle-rocker, quilt-maker, bread-baker, wife.
When she gave up wanderlust and the hour of the wolf,
settled for a white bed and fire in the hearth,
she sat before it unable to read the future in its flames.
Many chicks but one rooster, a shankbone in the pot.
Bottle-scrubber, boot-blacker, fresh-diaper, snot-wiper.
Floor-mopper, leaf-raker, candlestick-maker.
Gardener, scarecrow, drudge.  Berry-minder, button-finder.
Body-double, dreamer.  Sleep-walker, schemer.
Angel and whore.  Keeper of the flame.
Still, the bread wouldn't brown, jam wouldn't jell,
and, when the six-toed cat birthed a two-headed kitten,
lightning struck, leaving more fires to quench.
But as she beat at flames, her face was roughed
by fine grit, etching the spirit and the skin.

*To Dream of Black Swans Denotes Illicit Pleasures*

They were swimming in the lagoon, sculling
as they eased under the arched bridge reflected
among clouds on the still surface of morning.
Not a presence, more of an absence, empty space
where the sun was a ball of cold glass. Dark feathers
in the air, necks arched, mouths open, aching for
any tomorrow. A time of no time, mirrored eyes
reflecting only the present. Together, a sense of
burning – now, yet never again. Then water roiled,
lily pads entangled their feet, and a voice said,

"Stop this...." So she changed the dream, denied it,
ignored stone and leaf and glass,
reversed the negative, insisting and insisting
those sleek, insubstantial swans were always white.

*To Dream of Eating Vegetables*
*Is an Omen of Strange Luck*

*Showers of broken glass, gold and white,*
*yet wine-stained to the color of blood, splayed*
*around her as she tried to resist excess.*

First the leeks and eggplant, then the broccoli and a need
to cook and consume it. Brussels sprouts leeching water
an acrid brown or summer squash pulped into orange paste,
and she – who'd never liked vegetables –
was forking them into her mouth, greedy and heedless.

*Hearing discordant music, feeling the fire*
*of approaching change, she left*
*the tower but found herself in a labyrinth.*

As she knelt among carrots and parsnips, eager to taste
tops and all, she considered the stone, the leaf,
the unfound door, examined a bruise the shape of a moth
waiting for it to fly away. And when she looked up,
he was there – an almost-forgotten face – seasoned now,
heading down the road to where she knelt, his face
stenciled with morning light, arms heavy with strings
of bright peppers. "How did you find me?" she asked.
"And why have you come now?"

*While flaming slippers filled the air,*
*dark swans drifted by, and she breathed*
*the sharpness of onion and new Beaujolais.*

"To open the door," he said, festooning her with peppers
as they left the garden, the house with its empty bed
and cradle, wilting vegetables, bottle-splintered hearth.
Then, when he stroked her bruise with the tip of
his thumb, they crossed a threshhold,
stepped past leaf and stone, and began to dance.

**Notes**

Page 12 – "How many bees are there in a day" is a line from **The Book of Questions** by Pablo Neruda, translated by William O' Daly (Copper Canyon Press).

Page 28 – This poem refers to a large Louise Nevelson sculpture at the Museum of Modern Art in New York called "Sky Cathedral."

Page 29 – The some of the material for this poem was taken from **Gertrude Stein on Picasso** (W. W. Norton & Co.) and from an article by John Garth in the *Argonaut* called "Pablo Picasso – A Confession."

Page 40 – The title is a line from "Withered Compliments" by John Ashbery.

Page 54 – After a Marisol sculpture called "The Family" which is at the Museum of Modern Art in New York

Page 58 – This poem is a reply to a poem by Ahmed Arif called "In Jail."

Page 82 – "Fire is Favorable to the Dreamer:" The title and subtitles in this poem are taken from **Dreams A Book of Symbols** (Running Press Book Publishers).

**Recent Books by Susan Terris**

E YE OF THE H OLOCAUST , Arctos Press, 1999
C URVED S PACE , La Jolla Poets Press, 1998
N ELL'S Q UILT , Farrar, Straus & Giroux, 1996

**Recent Chapbooks**

S USAN T ERRIS : G REATEST H ITS , Pudding House Publications, 2000
A NGELS OF B ATAAN , Pudding House Publications, 1999

**Susan Terris** has had poetry published in *The Antioch Review, Ploughshares, Calyx, The Missouri Review, The Southern California Anthology, Poetry Northwest,* and dozens of other magazines and anthologies. FIRE IS FAVORABLE TO THE DREAMER is her second full-length book of poetry. In 2004, Adastra Press will publish a letterpress edition of her book POETIC LICENSE. In the last five years, her poems have won first prize in five national competitions and been nominated for 11 Pushcart Awards. Wth CB Follett, Ms. Terris is co-editor of *RUNES, A Review of Poetry.* She is also the author of 21 books of fiction. She lives in San Francisco with her husband David. To find out more about her, check out her web site: http://members.aol.com/sdt11.

**Special thanks** to CB Follett, Ruth Daigon, and Art Daigon for years of critiques, advice, enthusiasm, and for their on-going belief in my work as a poet.